Hope Soars
·······over·······
YELLOWSTONE

Written by Melissa C. Marsted • Illustrated by Cait Irwin
Designed by Aileen Aquino

Text and
Illustrations copyright © 2021
by Lucky Penny Publications, LLC. No part of this
publication may be reproduced, stored in a retrieval system,
or transmitted in any form or by any means, mechanical, photocopying,
recording, or otherwise without written permission from the publisher.

Cover and Book Design by Aileen Aquino

For inquiries or more information, email us at melissa@luckypennypress.com
or visit our website at www.luckypennypublications.com or our
Lucky Penny Publications Instagram account.

ISBN 978-1-938136-68-9

"For there is always light, if only we're brave enough to see it,

if only we're brave enough to be it."

Amanda Gorman

"To the children of our country, regardless of your gender, our country has sent you a clear message: Dream with ambition, lead with conviction, and see yourself in a way that others might not see you, simply because they've never seen it before. And we will applaud you every step of the way."

Vice President Kamala Harris

Welcome!

I'm Hope, a bald eagle and our country's national bird. It is with great honor that I will be your guide as I fly over the very first national park in the United States. Yellowstone National Park stretches into parts of three western states: Montana, Idaho and Wyoming.

Every year, here in Yellowstone, there are many wildfires. Some are caused by lightning, while others are caused by humans. Last year, I lost my favorite tree to a lightning strike, so I am searching for a new tree to call home. As I fly along my journey, I watch for signs of danger so I can warn the animals.

I'm going to head to Mammoth Hot Springs where we'll meet bison and grizzly bears. If we're lucky, we will spot endangered Rocky Mountain wolves, too.

Yellowstone is known for its geothermal activity. Some of the world's largest super volcanoes and geysers are found here. I am always on the lookout for signs of steam coming from inside the earth.

The parents of all the animals are working hard to protect their offspring from predators. They also teach them to find food to eat. Since I can soar high above the lands, I am able to swoop down and warn them if predators are lurking in the bushes.

MAMMOTH HOT SPRINGS

See those terraces? They are made from years of weather as water runs drop by drop over the soft limestone rock. The vibrant reds, oranges, yellows, and rosy pinks are created by bacteria, algae, and various mineral deposits.

Fish do not live in the geothermal pools. It is much too hot for them to survive. The water is heated from beneath the top layers of the earth. It then bubbles up and rises to the surface.

There are no trees to call home. I need to keep going.

Wheeeee!

LAMAR VALLEY

• • • • • • • • •

Lamar Valley is a wide open basin where many large mammals live. Look at the large herd of bison.

Bison are herbivores. They graze on grasses all day long. They can run fast and charge if they are scared or in danger. So watch out for their raised tails!

Bison are also very resilient. They can survive Yellowstone's harsh winters, finding food by sweeping snow out of the way with their strong shoulders.

"Hey there, Momma Bison. I know you are protecting your babies, but I can also keep my eyes on the lookout for danger. If I notice anything, I will warn you with my loud shrill."

Oh no! What's he doing? I better take a closer look.

Watch out! Watch out! Watch out!

Screeeechhh!

"Little one, I know you love to roll in the mud but did you look around? You have to watch out for the wolves, mountain lions, lynx, and bears. They are ready to pounce on you when you are wallowing in the dirt.

"See those gray wolves hiding over there? You have to pay attention. Wolves hunt in packs, so I am sure there are even more hiding in the bushes.

"Make sure you are always listening and smelling for danger. I'm trying to find a new home where I can feel safe, too, and be on the lookout for all of you."

I wasn't sure if we would spot a grizzly bear, but there's one with her two cubs. They were born while Momma Bear was hibernating in her winter den.

Black bears and grizzly bears are the only two species of bears that live in Yellowstone. One way to tell the difference is that grizzly bears have a large hump above their shoulders. They use this muscle and their long claws when they dig or forage for something yummy to eat like roots, insects, and other grubs in the dirt.

I am always on the watch to warn the cubs about any danger as I soar high above them.

LAMAR RIVER

Look over there. Two cubs are playing and trying to catch their own lunch. They love fishing for cutthroat trout, but they are not paying attention. I have to swoop down and warn them before the wolf charges after them.

There are so many different trees here - pine, fir, spruce, and aspen trees all grow here, but I haven't decided on which one to call my new home.

Time to explore!

ARTIST POINT

Here's Artist Point where I can see and hear the largest waterfall in Yellowstone. It's called Lower Falls, where the water drops more than 300 feet into the canyon and flows along the Yellowstone River. The height of Lower Falls would be like placing 50 bison one on top of another.

This feels like home, but with the sound of the crashing water, I would not be able to hear the animals if they need my help. I must keep soaring until I find the perfect tree.

Where, oh where is home?

Yellowstone caldera is one of the largest volcanoes in the world. If it erupts, all of the animals will have to flee. It can spew molten lava and ash for miles and miles.

I fly over all of Yellowstone to look for signs of an eruption or other dangers such as wildfires that might have been started by lightning or set by a human who was not careful.

It is my job to protect all of the animals, so I keep flying higher and higher. When it's time to warn the animals, I can dive 100 miles per hour.

This does not feel like a safe place for me to call home, so I am going to keep going.

NORRIS GEYSER BASIN

You know what that smell is? That's sulfur. It's a yellow element that is often found in places where there are hot springs and volcanoes. It is especially strong in this area of the park known as Norris Geyser Basin.

Look at that adorable black-footed ferret. He is endangered, which means he is at risk of becoming extinct. I need to check on him regularly but I really don't think I want to call this home. The smell is just too yucky for me to be able to sleep peacefully.

Stinky! Stinky! Stinky!

STEAMBOAT GEYSER

Before I leave, I'm going to check out Steamboat Geyser. Eruptions force water and steam from below the earth's surface 300 feet into the air. If we're lucky, we'll glimpse a rainbow as the sun's beams hit the vapor droplets. It's one of my favorite places to visit, but not to live.

When I notice danger, I can feel it in my feathers so I have to be able to take flight at a moment's notice. This spot is one of my favorite places to visit, but not to live. All the animals seem safe for now, so I'll keep going.

Up, Up, and Away and off I go!

GRAND PRISMATIC SPRING

Look at the rainbow of colors in this hot spring. Each ring represents different tiny living things called microbes. The center is too hot for them to survive, so the water is crystal clear. The edges are a bit cooler, but be careful! It's still too hot to touch.

Oh no! I see a wolf pup that strayed from its pack. She is about to take a sip from the spring. I must warn her right now!

Little pup, little pup! Stop! Don't touch!

Phew! That was close!

OLD FAITHFUL

I am getting tired, but I can't stop yet. I'll just take a short rest with all of my friends. My journey soaring above Yellowstone would not be complete until I experience the most famous geyser in the park.

Watch that spot over there. Any minute now it's going to blow water high, high into the air, as high as 140 feet. Old Faithful erupts below the earth's surface about 20 times per day.

I hear it starting to gurgle. It's getting louder and louder. There it goes!

Wasn't that amazing? I know for sure I love it here, but this is not home - not yet.

Follow me to my new home!

Today is my lucky day. We saw so many different kinds of animals that call Yellowstone National Park their home. I circled the caldera and visited some of Yellowstone's valleys, rivers, waterfalls, basins, geysers and hot springs.

All of the baby animals are quickly learning to pay attention using their five senses. Sight. Hearing. Smell. Taste. Touch. We must all learn to trust our intuition. It's that feeling when you know something is just right.

I used my five senses, but my intuition helped me make my final decision. I had hope. I had courage.

This feels right. This is home!

Time for me to take a rest while the park is quiet and peaceful. Ahhhh....

Good night my friends, good night!

Wildlife Adventures for Young Readers

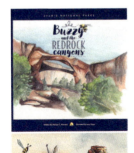

Buzzy and the Redrock Canyons
WRITTEN BY MELISSA C. MARSTED AND ILLUSTRATED BY IZZY GREER

Buzzy the bee zips across the state of Utah introducing readers to Utah's five national parks, starting with Arches, then continuing to Canyonlands, and finally crossing the state to Capitol Reef, Bryce Canyon, and Zion National Parks. Buzzy teaches readers about animals and endangered species that live in the parks as well as how arches, hoodoos, and spires were formed many years ago. *Buzzy and the Red Rock Canyons* is a great introduction to the wonders and magic of nature and the national parks system, originally established over 100 years ago.

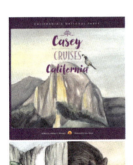

Casey Cruises California
WRITTEN BY MELISSA C. MARSTED AND ILLUSTRATED BY IZZY GREER

Readers join Casey, a California quail, on a journey through the nine national parks in his beautiful home state. Casey starts the adventure in the north at Redwoods National Park and narrates his way southward through forests with massive trees, majestic glacial formations, searing deserts, and sublime Pacific Islands, finally returning to the north to end his travels at Pinnacles National Park, and the Golden Gate Bridge, the world's gateway to California. Along the way Casey meets a variety of animal friends who help him understand the unique qualities of each park, and he also teaches readers some of the history and amazing fun facts about the parks.

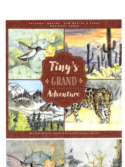

Tiny's Grand Adventure
WRITTEN BY MELISSA C. MARSTED AND ILLUSTRATED BY RUTHANNE HAMRICK

Join Tiny, a black-chinned hummingbird, as he travels across the American Southwest visiting eight national parks in Nevada, Arizona, New Mexico and Texas. Tiny meets many animal friends along the way; these friendships show us all that the differences between them are at the heart of the wonder of nature. It's a long journey for this little hummingbird, but as Tiny flies freely from place to place without borders or walls, he is proof positive that even the smallest of us can do big things.

The Secret Life of Phil
WRITTEN BY MELISSA C. MARSTED AND ILLUSTRATED BY CAIT IRWIN

The Secret Life of Phil explores the Black Hills of Wyoming and South Dakota through the journey of an endangered black-footed ferret. Phil encounters other endangered species and hides from predators in awe-inspiring places like Badlands National Park, Devils Tower National Monument, and Mount Rushmore National Memorial. The black-footed ferret is protected by the Endangered Species Act. Our story aims to raise awareness among our readers about endangered species and the important role we all play in protecting them. Most of all, *The Secret Life of Phil* seeks to inspire a sense of wonder about the beauty and magic of nature.

Molly's Tale of the American Pikas
WRITTEN BY MELISSA C. MARSTED AND ILLUSTRATED BY RUTHANNE HAMRICK

Molly the Meadowlark takes readers on a journey through five national parks that are currently threatened by climate change. Molly introduces us to the pika, an adorable mammal that can be found in each of the national parks Molly visits. Molly teaches young readers about pikas, including how they escape from other animals who hunt them. But what is an even greater danger to our pikas than all of these predators? Read *Molly's Tale of the American Pikas* to learn more about how changes in weather and climate are some of the biggest threats to the pika's way of life.

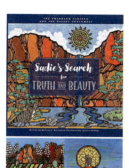

Sadie's Search for Truth and Beauty
WRITTEN BY MELISSA C. MARSTED AND ILLUSTRATED BY LYNETTE NICHOLS

Join Sadie, a greater sage-grouse, as she takes her three chicks throughout the Colorado Plateau and tells them stories about the ancient ruins and the magnificent rock formations that they encounter along the way. Sadie protects her chicks from the desert predators and teaches them how to search for water. On their journey, Sadie will reveal secrets to her chicks passed down by the Ancestral Puebloans. The chicks will learn survival skills. Will they find enough water to mature into adults? Open the pages filled with magical illustrations to learn more about the desert southwest.

Wildlife Adventures for Young Readers, continued

DeeDee's Year of Adventure
WRITTEN BY MELISSA C. MARSTED AND ILLUSTRATED BY CAIT IRWIN

Join DeeDee, a black-capped chickadee, as she begins her life learning to fly from her nest at the end of the spring. Her journey over, above and all around Acadia National Park, the only National Park in all of New England, takes her through the four seasons as she meets different animals along the way including a great blue heron, peregrine falcons, sand birds, a lobster, otters, a moose, a snowy owl and more. DeeDee knows she is in for a fluffy, white surprise, but only time will reveal the ultimate joy when she experiences what this means.

COMING IN 2021

Olé's Dark Sky Flight
WRITTEN BY MELISSA C. MARSTED AND ILLUSTRATED BY VICKI SPECK

For our newest book in our Wildlife Adventures for Young Readers series, Olé, an endangered Mexican spotted owl, begins his dark sky journey at Mesa Arch in Canyonlands NP. He observes a new constellation at each stop as he makes his way around the state of Utah, with one quick stop at Great Basin National Park in Nevada. The eight phases of the moon will also guide Olé along the way. Come along and enjoy where he soars through the dark, dark skies.

Valor and the National Seashore Horses
WRITTEN BY MELISSA C. MARSTED AND ILLUSTRATED BY AMANDA CHARLTON

Valor, a Shackleford foal, meets an egret named Ellie, who takes the readers on a journey along North Carolina's Outer Banks. She introduces the national seashores and the horses that have made their homes along the coast and explains how they have survived the hurricanes. Readers will soon feel the bond that is created between a bird and a foal as they begin their new lives and nature decides its course of action.

About the Designer

Aileen Aquino graduated with a BS in Visual Communication Design from The Ohio State University. She has been working at various design firms, architectural firms, and contemporary art museums for close to 20 years. Aileen specializes in print design and, in her free time, creates pieces for her own letterpress company in Salt Lake City. She enjoys exploring the outdoors with her two children – whether it's skiing, hiking, mountain biking, or climbing – and reveling in their awe of the world around them. She is passionate about designing books she can share with her children, who have inherited her love of books, art, and travel.

photo credit:
Jamie Lewis

photo credit:
Julie Buckles

About the Illustrator

Cait Irwin is a professional artist as well as a published author, activist, entrepreneur, naturalist, and world traveler. Being an artist and having a deep connection with the natural world are two major constants in her life. Her artwork spans a wide spectrum of media, styles, and subject matter.

A native of South Dakota, Cait graduated from Northland College in Wisconsin in 2003 with a BA in Studio Art with an emphasis in environmental studies. She stayed in the Northwoods area for several years, during which time she created murals, wrote a book, and taught herself woodworking. Cait eventually moved to Council Bluffs, Iowa to be closer to family and become a full-time artist. Seven years ago, she founded Irwin Artworks, LLC.

To learn more about Cait, visit her website www.irwinartworks.com. Her artwork is also available for purchase at www.etsy.com/shop/irwinartworks.

About Lucky Penny Publications

Dear Readers –

For as long as I can remember, I have loved to write, and I have loved to write letters. My second grade teacher at Cherry Brook Elementary School inspired my writing, creativity, and imagination. I started writing children's books nearly twenty years ago when my two sons were young boys.

Like Hope, the bald eagle, my family lost our home in the 2008 Santa Barbara Tea Fire and again evacuated for three days during the 2021 Parleys Canyon Fire. Also, like Hope, we moved eight times in four years after the fire until we found a new home in Park City, Utah. I started Lucky Penny Publications the year after the fire, but I didn't begin writing children's books about the national parks until early 2016. *Hope Soars over Yellowstone* is the eighth book in our Wildlife Adventures for Young Readers series. I am currently researching and writing about Utah's International Dark Sky Parks.

Last February, we had finally made a breakthrough with our sales to partner with Vacation Races at their series of half marathons in the national parks. We were so excited to have a booth at the Zion Half Marathon, and then the world experienced chaos. All of the races in 2020 were canceled.

Just like many people, I felt safest at home, venturing out to the grocery store, the gas station and the post office or for hikes and runs in nature, always with masks in hand. Our book projects kept me busy and focused on moving forward during all of 2020 and into 2021.

As we finished *DeeDee's Year of Adventure*, I had the chance to visit Yellowstone National Park and plan Hope's journey. A bald eagle was an easy choice as our main character - our national bird. Hope represents safety and security for all of the animals in the park. I wanted the animals to trust her. For me, a soaring bird symbolizes freedom. With life's trials and tribulations, nature never disappoints and almost always inspires.

That is my hope, too - that our books are fun, educational, and inspirational. The more you notice, the more nature will send you messages.

Nature is everywhere for all of us to enjoy.

All my best,

Melissa Marsted

About the Author

photo credit:
Peter Marsted

Melissa grew up in a small town in northwestern Connecticut where she built forts in the woods and picked wild raspberries. Her second grade teacher inspired her lifelong love of writing. After losing her house in the Santa Barbara Tea Fire in 2008, she self-published her first children's book and started Lucky Penny Publications. She relocated to Utah in 2013 and began writing children's books about the national parks in 2016. An avid long-distance runner, she creates her books by running along the same trails as the animals she writes about in her books. She believes that being in nature is where the magic of synchronicity and creativity happens.
Instagram @*luckypennypublications*.

"If a child is to keep alive an inborn sense of wonder ...

the child needs the companionship of at least one adult who can share it, rediscovering

with that child the joy, excitement, and mystery of the world we live in."

Rachel Carson

Fun Facts
Yellowstone National Park

- In 1872, Ulysses S. Grant, the 18th President, signed the Yellowstone National Park Protection Act to establish Yellowstone National Park and to protect the area as public lands for all people. Sequoia National Park was established in 1890, followed by Yosemite in 1890 and Mount Rainer in 1899.

- Over two million acres comprise this national park that stretches into parts of three states: Montana, Idaho and Wyoming. The total area of Yellowstone is bigger than the two smallest states, Rhode Island and Delaware, combined.

- Over 300 species of birds, 16 types of fish and 67 different species of mammals live in Yellowstone.

- Bison live in the United States, and buffalo live in Asia and Africa. Bison also have thick beards while buffalo do not. Yellowstone is the only location where bison have lived (without interruption) since prehistoric times.

- Baby bison are called red dogs because of their red fur at birth that darkens as they mature.

- After reintroducing the gray wolf back into Yellowstone in 1995, as of January 2020 almost 100 wolves and eight packs live in Yellowstone National Park and can be seen in the Lamar Valley region.

- Over 700 grizzly bears reside in Yellowstone National Park and as of 2018 are currently on the list of endangered species.

- The Yellowstone River runs 700 miles from North Dakota until it reaches the Missouri River, then flows into the Mississippi before it finally empties in the Gulf of Mexico near Louisiana. It is the longest unobstructed river in the lower 48 states.

- A portion of the Continental Divide runs through Yellowstone where rivers on the west side of the Divide flow into the Pacific Ocean and the rivers on the east side flow into the Atlantic Ocean.

- Situated over 7,700', Yellowstone Lake is the largest high-elevation lake in North America. It is roughly 20 miles long and 14 miles wide, with 141 miles of shoreline. There are more than 600 lakes and ponds that can be found in Yellowstone National Park. There are almost 300 waterfalls that can be found in Yellowstone.

- The Yellowstone Caldera, which first erupted 650,000 years ago, measures 30 by 45 miles.

- There are more than 500 active geyers in Yellowstone. The eruption of Old Faithful happens every 60 to 110 minutes and roughly 17 times each day. When it erupts, it forces between 4,000 and 8,000 gallons of water into the air.

- The park rangers predict that if the eruption lasts less than two and a half minutes, then it will take 60 minutes until Old Faithful erupts again. If it is longer than that, then the next eruption will probably take place in about 90 minutes.

For more information about Wildlife Adventures for Young Readers or Lucky Penny Publications, please email us at melissa@luckypennypress.com. For updates on our newest books, please click on our website www.luckypennypublications.com or our Instagram @luckypennypublications.

Made in the USA
Middletown, DE
17 February 2022